The WATER in BETWEEN

A Photographic Celebration of Lake Champlain

The WATER in BETWEEN

A Photographic Celebration of Lake Champlain

HUNTINGTON GRAPHICS

Shelburne, Vermont

Published by Huntington Graphics, PO Box 373, Burlington, VT 05402
www.huntingtongraphics.com
Printed in the U.S.A. by J.S. McCarthy Printers, Augusta, ME

Compiled by Jared Gange
Designed by Andrea Gray
Text by Emery Hard
Cover photo: *On the Wind* by John David Geery, the Burlington waterfront at dusk
Back cover photo: Robert Lyons, Camels Hump at sunset
Technical support and design by John Hadden
Photo assistance by Kerrie Morrison Pughe
Dust jacket map by Northern Cartographic, South Burlington, VT

ISBN 978-1-886064-35-5

First edition

Contents

Sponsors

HANSON | Investment Management

Preface

*T*he year 2009 marks the 400th anniversary of the European discovery of Lake Champlain. In conjunction with the many Quadricentennial events and heightened awareness of the Lake and the surrounding region, it seems fitting to create a visual celebration of the Lake and the Lake Champlain Basin. *The Water In Between* brings together the work of over thirty photographers, from Vermont, New York and Québec.

This book reaches beyond the shores and body of the lake to its sources in the surrounding mountains and the human activities within its hundreds of miles of watershed area. Lake Champlain boasts a rich history and present-day variety that ranges from wilderness to bustling cities.

Lake Champlain is seen more and more as a national treasure, a superb recreation destination offering world-class mountain and lake views. And for those of us lucky enough to live here, the region offers a quality of life that is consistently recognized as one of the best in the country.

— Jared Gange
May 2009

PERSPECTIVES

*S*tretching over two countries and two U.S. states, Lake Champlain is the largest body of freshwater in America after the Great Lakes. At its extremes, the lake is 12 miles wide, 400 feet deep, and extends northward 120 miles from the basin near Whitehall, New York to its outlet in Québec. From the Narrows in the south, where the Champlain Canal begins its path to the Hudson River, the lake widens into the Broad Lake midway up its length. North of Burlington, Vermont's Champlain Islands command the waters. By the time it reaches the Richelieu River, a tributary of the St. Lawrence, Lake Champlain has passed by the forts and ruins of its early settlement, and over the bateaux that sank in the fight for its possession. Its waters have nourished the crops along its banks, and provided habitat for fish, birds, and mammals. In its slow journey to the Atlantic, the lake flows from thousands of faucets, while also providing a playground for swimmers, sailors, and fishermen. As both a grave for its history and a stage for its present, Lake Champlain touches the lives of residents and visitors alike.

▶ *Whallons Bay looking toward Giant Mountain. Essex, New York.*

Shelburne Inn from Lone Tree Hill. Shelburne Farms, Vermont.

A flaming evening sky from Mount Philo, Vermont.

Aerial view of the well-protected bay known as the "Gut." North Hero, Champlain Islands, Vermont.

Juniper Island and the Four Brothers Islands, looking west toward the Adirondacks.

Looking southeast across the Burlington harbor with Vermont's iconic Camels Hump in the distance.

From Sunset Ledge, Lake Champlain is just a sliver in the distance. Lincoln Gap, Vermont.

Canada geese rest in the evening calm. Thompson's Point, Charlotte, Vermont.

Lake Champlain and the Adirondacks provide a world-class sunset.

Approaching the historic hamlet of Essex on the Charlotte-Essex ferry.

Looking south from Isle la Motte on a warm summer day. Champlain Islands, Vermont.

Aerial view of New York's Fort Ticonderoga. International Paper's mill is visible in the distance.

New York's Poke-O-Moonshine Mountain gives a sweeping view of Lake Champlain and the mountains on the Vermont side.

Just north of the border, Fort Lennox was built in the 1800s to protect the British colony from a possible American invasion. Richelieu River, Québec.

SOURCES

Although Lake Champlain covers a large area of the Northeast—490 square miles, 55 of which are islands —the lake's watershed dwarfs its dimensions. Nestled between New York's Adirondacks and the Green Mountains of Vermont, Lake Champlain drains more than 8,200 square miles of forest, wetlands, and open fields. From the east, these slopes feed rivers like the Missisquoi, Lamoille, Winooski, and Otter Creek. From the west, New York's Chazy, Saranac, Ausable, Salmon, and Boquet Rivers deliver the mountains' rain and snow to the lake. The Ausable even travels through a deep chasm two miles long, still carving a course through the sandstone after thousands of years. To the south, not only the Poultney and Mettawee Rivers, but Lake George itself drains into the lake. In fact, the Lake Champlain Basin extends into the Northeast Kingdom of Vermont and westward as far as Saranac Lake. With its great reach, Lake Champlain defines the history and culture of a region far beyond sight of its shores.

▶ *The Winooski River's serpentine finale. Burlington, Vermont.*

Beautiful and unusual, Lake Placid reveals itself best from above. The village of Lake Placid is in the foreground, Whiteface Mountain is in the distance.

Ski runs, slide scars, and the road to the summit are all visible in this aerial view of Whiteface Mountain. Lake Placid is in the distance.

Mount Mansfield's Lake of the Clouds is one of the highest sources of Lake Champlain.

A mountain stream begins its long journey to the Lake.

This huge swamp resides in a low spot on the spine of the Green Mountains. Nebraska Notch, Vermont.

High in the Adirondacks, Mary Louise Pond basks in autumn colors.

The Ausable River in winter dress, near Keene Valley, New York.

Early-morning light on Dead Creek. Addison, Vermont.

This little stream feeds Lake Champlain near Valcour Island. Peru, New York.

New York's Lake George drains north into Lake Champlain. This view is from Tongue Mountain.

ON the LAKE

Since the golden era of steam power, when barges transported products like lumber, livestock, textiles, and iron ore between Canada and the northeastern United States, Lake Champlain has evolved into a mecca for recreation. Although its waters still facilitate travel, even commuting, between New York and Vermont, as commerce moved onto the highways, the lake blossomed with much smaller vessels. In the summer, popular activities include fishing, sailing, swimming, water-skiing, kayaking, canoeing, and even dragon boat racing. The schooner *Lois McClure*, a replica of a nineteenth-century canal boat, also floats alongside the modern pleasure boats. In the winter months, when much of the lake lies frozen, ice fishing shanties appear in many bays, and skaters glide over windblown patches of clear ice. From north to south, plentiful harbors, state parks, and public beaches provide access to Lake Champlain's many possibilities. In all seasons, those who venture offshore enjoy a diverse array of activities and weather, from the hunter shooting mallards from his blind to the ferry breaking a path through the February ice.

▶ *A sailboat is dwarfed by Giant Mountain, an Adirondack High Peak.*

Wakeboard acrobatics on a hot summer day.

Training for the annual Dragon Boat Festival in the Burlington harbor.

After weathering the storm, these sailors get a stunning visual treat. Shelburne Bay, Vermont.

Kayakers stick close to shore as a summer thunderstorm builds to the west. Cedar Beach, Charlotte, Vermont.

Contestants in the annual Lake Champlain International Fishing Derby head out in the early morning to try their luck. Plattsburgh, New York.

Ice formations along the shore frame ice fishermen and their shanties.

Spinnakers catch the evening breeze. Shelburne Bay, Vermont

A cooling dip on a warm summer evening.

The Adirondack, *the oldest of the Lake Champlain ferries, labors in autumn waves. Off Essex, New York.*

Ice-fishing shanties near the Crown Point Bridge.

At high speed in an ice boat regatta.

An ice-skater enjoys spectacular light off Shelburne Point.

Canoeing in choppy water off Shelburne Point, with Dunder Rock and Juniper Island in the background.

The Charlotte-Essex ferry navigates an open lead in late winter.

Boats put up for the season at Gagnon Marina. Richelieu River, Saint-Paul-de-l'Île-aux-Noix, Québec.

A kayaker enjoys the calm, glassy surface. Crown Point Bridge is in the distance.

Dark clouds portend a stormy night. Charlotte, Vermont.

Captain Alan Wood enjoys a calm and clear evening on the Charlotte-Essex crossing.

This lightweight canoe is almost transparent. Valcour Island, New York.

From Whitehall, New York, the Champlain Canal leads south to the Hudson River.

Onboard the Lois McClure, *a replica of an 1862-class sailing canal boat.*

The Lois McClure gets an assist from a tugboat. Vermont's Camels Hump is in the background.

STONE, WOOD, and STEEL

Among the oldest structures on Lake Champlain are the French and British forts, including Ticonderoga, built during the two centuries of struggle over this strategic corridor. Eroded by time, weather, and enemy gunpowder, only ruins remain on Crown and Chimney Points, though stones taken from the forts still exist in the area's first houses. To the north, the principal cities of Burlington and Plattsburgh enjoyed a long history of commerce and industry before becoming centers of business, education, and tourism. Many small towns also attract visitors while maintaining their agricultural roots. The southernmost lake crossing is the seasonal Larrabee's Point ferry between Ticonderoga and Shoreham, while northern commuters may ride the Grand Isle–Plattsburgh ferry throughout the year. While only the Crown Point Bridge spans the entire lake, several others connect the Champlain Islands to the mainland. This network of ferries and bridges provides a close relationship between neighboring states, as Lake Champlain continues to be a magnet for the region's population.

▶ *Rouse's Point Bridge links the island of North Hero to New York.*

These cabins evoke an earlier time. On US Route 2, North Hero, Vermont.

The heart of the Middlebury College campus.

Fort Ticonderoga, New York, at the southern end of the Lake, was strategically important during 18th-century conflicts.

The University of Vermont quad, facing Williams Hall and the Old Mill Building.

Early-evening light on a summer camp. Starr Farm, Burlington.

Burlington with the University of Vermont on the hilltop. Mount Mansfield, Vermont's highest mountain, is in the background.

Vermont's second-largest city, Rutland, nestles at the foot of the Green Mountains.

The stupendous Farm Barn at Shelburne Farms. Shelburne, Vermont.

The Burlington Bike Path Bridge crosses the Winooski River right at its mouth.

Sunset glow at the Burlington Boathouse.

The Colchester Reef Lighthouse is in retirement at the Shelburne Museum.

This 19th-century lake steamer, the Ticonderoga, *provides a fascinating glimpse of a bygone era. Shelburne Museum, Vermont.*

For almost 200 years the Essex Inn has welcomed guests. Essex, New York.

Gulls wait expectantly by the ferry dock. The Old Dock Restaurant, Essex, New York.

Out for an evening sail on a brisk northerly breeze. Burlington Breakwater.

The signature Adirondack chairs of the Basin Harbor Club. Ferrisburgh, Vermont.

The stone for this historic home was dragged across the ice from nearby Isle la Motte. North Hero, Vermont.

A fine summer day. Charlotte, Vermont.

The Ausable River slips through the little town of Keeseville, New York.

An historic train station on the Albany-Montreal line. Westport, New York.

Church Street is dressed up for Christmas. Burlington, Vermont.

The ECHO Lake Aquarium and Science Center at the Leahy Center for Lake Champlain. Burlington waterfront.

OFF the LAKE

*I*n addition to its wealth of water activities, the Lake Champlain Basin offers many ways to enjoy the lake from afar. Hikers and snowshoers walk beside the watershed's fledgling streams while climbing the peaks of the Green Mountains or Adirondacks. Skiers often pause at the top of their runs to gaze at the sparkling sliver of lake in the distance. From low vistas like Snake Mountain, one sees the open fields of the Champlain Valley, where many farms use the fertile soil along the lakeshore to grow hay, grains, vegetables, and fruits. Apple orchards abound most famously in Shoreham, Vermont, where blossoms scent the air in spring and fruit ripens with the colors of autumn. The natural beauty surrounding Lake Champlain draws students to nearby colleges, while also providing a backdrop for annual sporting events like the Lake Champlain International Fishing Derby and the Vermont City Marathon. As the focal point of everything from the 20-mile bike path that runs along its banks to the sweeping estate of Shelburne Farms, Lake Champlain lies at the center of a vibrant local culture.

▶ *A great view from Snake Mountain. Addison County, Vermont.*

The Champlain Valley Fair marks the end of summer. Essex Junction, Vermont.

The Causeway, an old railroad bed linking Burlington and Colchester with the Champlain Islands, is now part of the Burlington Bike Path.

Apple orchards in spring. Shelburne Orchards, Vermont.

A spring baseball game in Charlotte, Vermont.

Hikers descend from the summit of Mount Marcy, New York's highest peak.

These hikers have just reached the summit of Stowe Pinnacle. Stowe, Vermont.

Snowboarder on the summit of Mount Mansfield. Lake Champlain and the Adirondacks are in the distance.

A solitary biker enjoys a peaceful back road in the shadow of Mount Mansfield. Cambridge, Vermont.

Almost there, hikers approach the summit of Mount Mansfield.

Rafting down the spectacular Ausable Chasm, New York.

Riders in the Women's Pro class in the Burlington Criterium zip around the one-kilometer circuit in downtown Burlington.

The annual Burlington City Marathon attracts thousands of runners of all abilities.

Headed for the sun on Mad River Glen's historic single-chair ski lift. Mad River Valley, Vermont.

A skier takes an extreme line off the summit of Mount Mansfield.

Blazing down a run at Sugarbush Ski Resort. Warren, Vermont.

Bird houses on South Hero, Champlain Islands.

A lonely hay wagon glows in the evening light. Shoreham, Vermont.

Boiling sap at the Taft sugarhouse in Huntington, Vermont.

Annual Mozart Festival concert at Shelburne Farms.

Paddling down the Mad River. Waitsfield, Vermont.

Seagulls manage to glean an early harvest during spring plowing.

These fields have been readied for winter. Essex, New York.

REFLECTIONS

From its sandy beaches and verdant meadows to the rugged, alpine peaks of the Adirondacks, the Lake Champlain Basin offers a landscape for one's every whim. A hiker may wake early to see the sun rise over the lake, while a fisherman may bait his lines for bullheads as dusk creeps onto a pond. A forester can cruise a mature stand of maples, while a dairy farmer pastures his cows on a lush field of alfalfa. The region's allure is no secret, as people from all over the world travel here to see the vibrant fall foliage, tour the cities and towns, and tackle the wealth of outdoor activities. With a diverse array of museums, resorts, parks, and trails, the basin invites visitors to immerse themselves in the region's past, while enjoying the momentary pleasures of the present. While some people travel to every corner of this great watershed, others simply stroll along the bike path past sparkling granite boulders, past a web of icicles cast up by the waves, slowly melting in the winter sun.

▶ *Looking into the sunset, across Appletree Point from Burlington.*

Strong sunset colors reflected on Keeler Bay. Grand Isle, Vermont.

Geometric chunks of ice covered with new snow on Shelburne Point.

Water creates its own artistry.

Looking toward Plattsburgh from Phelps Point on a summer evening. Grand Isle, Vermont.

The surprising flatness of the Champlain Islands.

Autumn colors are reflected in Waterbury Reservoir, Vermont.

Lightning illuminates Shelburne Bay while Burlington creates its own glow.

Fourth of July fireworks over Malletts Bay, Vermont.

PASSAGES

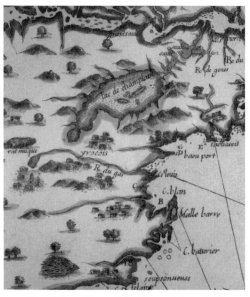

Detail from Samuel de Champlain's 1612 map of New France.

*B*efore Samuel de Champlain claimed the lake for France in 1609, the native Abenaki called it *Petonbowk*, meaning "waters that lie between." Although Lake Champlain defines the boundary between Vermont and New York, it unites even as it divides, reaching over the Canadian border. Today, people on both sides of the immense watershed enjoy the natural beauty and rich cultural heritage of the region.

Geology and Physical Geography

Although the quadricentennial of Samuel de Champlain's journey into the Champlain Valley celebrates a great landmark in the region's past, the physical forces that shaped Lake Champlain began long before humans appeared. Half a billion years ago, the nascent domes of the Adirondacks stood to the west of a saltwater trough called the Iapetus Ocean. When the earth's crust convulsed once again, forcing the ocean's sedimentary rocks upward to create both the 400 million-year-old Taconics and Green Mountains, the upheaval forced the saltwater back northward. With the onset of the Great Ice Age 20,000 years ago, glaciers advanced into the region, eroding and weathering the mountains into their rounded, present-day forms.

As the earth began to warm 7,500 years later, the one-mile thick ice sheet that covered the Northeast slowly melted into Lake Vermont. This large body of freshwater lapped at the feet of the Green Mountains for 2,500 years before the retreating glacier opened a path for saltwater from the St. Lawrence estuary to rush in. For the next 1,000 years the Champlain Sea, a wing of the Atlantic, teemed with oceanic animals like cod, seals, blue mussels, and beluga whales. In 1849, one of these whale skeletons surfaced in Charlotte during excavations for a new railway. The modern contours of Lake Champlain did not appear until the land rebounded from the burden of heavy glacial ice, expelling the saltwater once again, and rainfall allowed a new freshwater ecosystem to evolve.

Today, 9,000 years after its birth, Lake Champlain covers 435 square miles and averages over 6 cubic miles in volume. The lake's long, narrow body stretches 120 miles from the basin at Whitehall, New York to its outlet in Québec. During this slow journey northward to the Richelieu River—a tributary of the St. Lawrence—the lake varies so greatly in width and depth that geographers divide it into five distinct segments. At the southern tip, where the man-made Champlain Canal deposits its freight from the Hudson River, the South Lake marks a narrow boundary between Vermont and New York. Champlain then opens into the Broad Lake near Charlotte, Vermont and Essex, New York, where the water plunges to its greatest depth of 400 feet. At its widest point—the twelve miles between Burlington and Port Kent—the lake usually freezes around February 12th, though this unbroken sheet of ice has formed less reliably in recent years, freezing across only three winters between 1990 and 2000.

Farther north, the Champlain Islands split the Broad Lake into three segments that lie mostly within Vermont's borders: Malletts Bay, the Inland Sea, and Missisquoi Bay. At only 15 feet deep, the latter region, which straddles

The lake was born with the passing of the Great Ice Age.

Franklin County and Québec, falls far short of the lake's average depth of 64 feet. While the dimensions of ancient Lake Vermont dwarf those of the modern lake, Champlain earned the status of the sixth Great Lake for a short time in 1998. Although this official status was revoked, the lake remains a unique body of water for its great size, dramatic geological and human histories, and immense watershed.

The Lake Champlain Basin reaches far beyond the lake's 587 miles of shoreline. Bordered to the south by the Hudson River Basin and to the east by the Connecticut River Basin, the lake's watershed covers 8,234 square miles—56% of which are in Vermont, 37% in New York, and 7% in the Canadian province of Québec. Both the rugged Adirondacks, which continue to rise five million years after their first upward stirrings, and the lower Green Mountains of Vermont feed the headwaters of the major rivers that drain into Lake Champlain. To the west, the basin extends as far as Saranac Lake; in the east, portions of Vermont's Northeast Kingdom add their rainfall to streams destined for the lake. Even Lake George eventually flows into Champlain.

Most of this great basin falls into five regions: the Champlain Lowlands, the Adirondacks, the Green Mountains, the Taconic Mountains, and the Valley of Vermont—a small agricultural area between the Taconics and the Green Mountains. Two smaller sub-basins—the Vermont Piedmont at the far eastern edge of the watershed, and the Hudson Valley in the southwestern corner of the range—also contribute their waters to America's sixth largest lake. Each of these

The cliffs in Willsboro Bay, New York.

Great Chazy, and Ausable. In the years between falling as rain and entering the Atlantic, these waters nourish the region's trees, crops, wildlife, livestock, and more than half a million people who call the Lake Champlain Basin home.

Covering an area about 85% the size of Vermont, Lake Champlain's watershed provides habitat for an abundance of plant and animal life. From the agricultural fields and meadows of the lowlands, the land transitions to deciduous forests full of deer, coyotes, beavers, porcupines, and fisher cats, as well as many bird species. At higher elevations, these broad-leaved forests give way to spruce-fir ecosystems—prime habitat for moose, pine martens, and snowshoe hares. In the Adirondacks and on a few of Vermont's highest peaks, small patches of alpine tundra support dwarf vegetation and tolerant animal species like voles, shrews, and red squirrels. The Lake Champlain Basin also includes 300,000 acres of wetlands, which provide essential habitat for many species, and also improve water quality by removing excess nutrients, processing wastes, and trapping sediments. As part of the Atlantic Flyway corridor, the basin's wetlands provide a place for birds to rest and feed during their fall and spring

migrations. Several fish species such as northern pike, black bullhead, and yellow perch also depend on these wetlands for their spawning grounds.

Combined with this great variety of natural habitat, the dramatic geological history of Lake Champlain defines its unique physical character. Both the ancient marine fossils of Chazy Reef and the carnivorous pitcher plants that live in bogs lie within the same watershed. The series of glacial changes that repeatedly tipped the balance between saltwater and freshwater also left a legacy of mountains, hills, fault blocks, rounded valleys, sandstone and limestone, and younger metamorphic rock. As the culmination of these eons of rumblings, the glaciers

Pitcher plants abound in the basin's wetlands.

sub-basins contains at least one tributary fed by countless small streams. Of the rivers that drain directly into the lake, the largest are the Otter Creek, Missisquoi, Winooski, Lamoille, Mettawee, Lewis Creek, and Poultney in Vermont, as well as New York's Saranac, Boquet, created the lakebed itself—the destination of all those quadrillions of gallons of water.

History

The first people to inhabit the Champlain Valley arrived more than 11,000 years ago, as the Laurentian Glacier retreated northward and the last ice age came to an end. These Paleo-Indians likely migrated across the land bridge from Siberia to Alaska, traveled south to the American Midwest, then branched off to the northeast, where a group settled on the shores of the Champlain Sea. Finding plentiful herds of mastodons, woolly mammoths, and caribou to hunt, these prehistoric people roamed the tundra following their prey. As the climate warmed and forests encroached upon the open plains during the next several thousand years, a new type of Native American—the Archaic People—replaced its nomadic forbearer. The lives of these small game hunters and fishermen centered on watersheds and the lake that connected them. In turn, the Woodland People who appeared 3,000 years ago grew even more sedentary, practicing horticulture on the flood plains of major rivers like the Winooski. Evidence of large flint quarries near both St. Albans Bay and Mount Independence indicate trade between tribes and the construction of stone implements and weapons.

Stone inscriptions, Crown Point, New York.

By the time of European contact, the St. Lawrence Iroquois, Western Abenaki, Mahican, and Mohawk tribes all called the Champlain Valley home. Despite the Native Americans' ancient claims to the land and watercourses, the events that began four hundred years ago drastically changed the region's cultural landscape.

In the age of early American settlement, the first successful trans-Atlantic voyages inspired many Europeans to exploit the New World's valuable natural resources and to tame its vast wilderness. Although the first white man to claim the Champlain Valley paddled up the lake more than a century after Columbus landed in the Bahamas, the region soon vaulted to the center of colonial conflict. Samuel de Champlain was born in Brouage, France in 1567, the son of a sea captain and nephew of a navel officer. With the ocean in his blood, he first sailed abroad at the age of twenty-two, exploring the West Indies, Central America, Mexico, and the coast of New England before traveling to the St. Lawrence Valley in 1608, where he founded the first French colony that survived in North America. There, in what is now Québec City, Champlain agreed to accompany his Algonquin, Huron, and Montagnais allies southward to battle their enemies on the "Sea of the Iroquois."

In the summer of 1609, the war party of sixty Native Americans and three Europeans traveled up the Richelieu River and onto the lake in twenty-four canoes, thus entering waters that Jacques Cartier had perhaps glimpsed from atop Mount Royal, but no white man had yet visited. After several weeks of paddling they found the enemy Iroquois and soon engaged in battle—a contest that the Algonquin easily won with their European companions' firearms. Although he never returned to the lake after giving it his name, Samuel de Champlain left his mark on the Champlain Valley, not only for recording its "discovery" in great detail, but for his precise actions remembered: "I promised the [Algonquin] to do all in my power [to kill the chiefs] and said that I was very sorry that they could not understand me well, so that I might give order and system to their attack of the enemy." Champlain's voyage on the "Sea of the Iroquois" colored the centuries of European conflict that followed, for the tribe he attacked with his arquebus forever hated the French and sided with Britain in the wars to come.

Soon after Champlain traveled the lake for France, Henry Hudson claimed the unseen area to the north of the Hudson River while exploring for the Dutch East India Company in September of 1609. Spurred by European fashion's thirst for beaver pelts, neither nation would relinquish its designs on the resources of the New World until the British captured New Amsterdam in 1664 and inherited the Dutch claims. At first Britain used its Iroquois allies to fight the French, trading raids up and down the lake between Albany and Canada. Often

marching in winter, many men on both sides died of cold, starvation, "snow-shoe sickness," and ambush, forced to retreat across the frozen lake before they even reached the enemy fort or village. By 1690, Britain itself had entered the fray as King William's War drifted across the Atlantic and stirred the colonists to new violence. Even though the Treaty of Utrecht, signed in April of 1713, split the lake between competing nations, France and Britain never agreed upon the boundary line and continued to fight for control of the Champlain Valley. In turn, Queen Anne's War (1702–13), King

Shipwrecks from every era of Lake Champlain's maritime heritage can be found on the floor of lake.

George's War (1744–48), and the French and Indian War (1755–63) revived hostilities after short periods of peace.

Since each successive treaty ending these European wars failed to clarify sovereignty over the colonies, both the French and the British built forts and amassed supplies throughout the mid-eighteenth century. Britain built its first outpost on Lake Champlain on Chimney Point, a narrow part of the lake called Pointe a la Chevelure by the French, perhaps named for the scalps that Champlain's war party took from their Iroquois victims. Although this particular fort fell into French hands in 1731 and was later burned, this part of the lake remained a strategic stronghold throughout the next century of war. In 1734 the King of France chose Crown Point, directly across the lake from Chimney Point, for the site of Fort St. Frederic—a four-story stone citadel that protected the community that grew up around it, stored supplies for military campaigns, and proved a symbolic reminder of France's claims to the Champlain Valley.

After losing the Battle of Lake George, an ill-conceived attack on Fort Edward, Governor Vaudreuil of Québec ordered a new fort to be built farther south on a high promontory overlooking the lake. As a staging area for attacks on British positions near Lake George, Fort

Carillon fell short of France's ambitions of conquest. Although a large French force led by General Louis Joseph de Montcalm managed to capture Fort William Henry in July of 1757 and then repelled General James Abercromby's retaliation against Carillon the following year, the fort that later became Ticonderoga fell in a three-day siege by the British General Jeffery Amherst in 1759, and burned at the hands of its own light garrison before the soldiers retreated north. Chased back to Canada, the French could only surrender and await the Treaty of Paris of 1763, which formally gave Britain control of a large portion of North America. Though severely damaged by fire, Fort Ticonderoga continued to change hands in the ongoing struggle for Lake Champlain—a key waterway for both naval strategy and access to the fertile land along its shores.

Despite official British sovereignty over most territory south of the St. Lawrence, land disputes continued to plague the area after the French and Indian War. Both Governor Wentworth of New Hampshire and Governors Colden and Tryon of Albany, New York issued charters for parcels of the New Hampshire Grants—the land between Lake Champlain and the Connecticut River that

The Richelieu River rushes by Chambly Fort, en route to the St. Lawrence.

is now the state of Vermont. Often, new settlers would arrive at their grant only to find a community of houses, roads, and mills already under construction. In this contest between colonial governments, Ethan Allen and his

militia of Green Mountain Boys physically secured the Grants for New Hampshire settlers, while Governor Wentworth also helped his case by granting land to the Church of England and thus drawing King George III over to his side. New York had little chance to retaliate, as Britain's attention soon turned to the greater rebellion brewing in America.

Not long after Britain wrested the colonies away from France, its settlers began to chafe against the strict laws and taxes of the absentee monarchy. With the initial shots of the Revolutionary War, the patriots realized that they needed stronger artillery to withstand the professional British army. Ethan Allen understood the gravity of these nascent events when he resolved to fix his energy on a foe more dangerous than the royal governors of New York, explaining that, "the first systematical and bloody attempt, at Lexington, to enslave America, thoroughly electrified my mind, and fully determined me to take part with my country." With the goal of securing arms for the patriots, both Ethan Allen and Benedict Arnold conspired to capture Fort Ticonderoga—now a lightly occupied British armory that had greatly decayed since Amherst's attempts to rebuild it.

With permission from the congresses of Connecticut and Massachusetts, a force of two hundred Green Mountain Boys gathered in Hand's Cove (Shoreham, Vermont) on May 11, 1775, though only eighty rowed across the lake in time to witness the swift surrender of the British soldiers. According to legend, Allen surprised the Commandant in his bedchamber by banging on the door and crying, "Come out of there, you damned old rat!" After this victory, the rebels captured the fort at Crown Point and then took the loyalist town of Skenesborough, New York, later renamed Whitehall. Though happy to have Ticonderoga's cannon for the siege of Boston that winter, Congress was unprepared for the implications of this aggression and would have relinquished the forts if Allen and Arnold had not argued for the protection of the families living along the lake.

After much delay and uncertainty, the government also agreed to mount a three-pronged attack on the British forces stationed in Canada, hoping to convince Canadian civilians to join the rebellion. Despite an initial success in Montréal, the Americans failed in their siege

French and Indian Wars re-inactment at Fort Ticonderoga.

of Québec and were devastated by smallpox during their retreat. With only four captured British ships, the weak, disease-ravaged Americans managed to hold the lake while both sides rushed to construct naval fleets for the inevitable battles ahead. Over the next few months, Benedict Arnold oversaw the feverish construction of his ships and organized the grueling journey of their rigging and weaponry overland.

Since the Americans would surely face a superior fleet, Arnold planned a defensive strategy, concealing his sixteen ships in the narrow channel between Valcour Island and the western shore of Lake Champlain. On October 11, 1776, the enemy sailed up the Broad Lake and approached the Americans from the south, as predicted, where favorable autumn winds helped Arnold engage the British until nightfall. Unwilling to accept the defeat inevitable at first light, the Americans escaped southward in the foggy darkness, only to renew the battle when the British discovered the trick in the morning. Eventually, Arnold's heavy losses forced him to run his remaining ships aground at what is now Arnold's Bay, in Panton, Vermont, and to escape overland to Crown Point. While the British took the fort there, Fort Ticonderoga resisted siege and its assailants returned to Canada for the winter. Regardless of the contest's outcome, the Battle of Valcour Island demonstrated the determination and strength of the Americans in the face of a superior force.

Although General Sir John Burgoyne invaded the Champlain Valley in June of 1777 and hauled his cannon up Mount Defiance, forcing the American General St. Clair to abandon Fort Ticonderoga and Mount Independence without firing a shot, the British soon began to lose ground in the colonies. After one more British victory at the Battle of Hubbardton, the monarchy lost at Bennington, and again in two battles at Freeman's Farm, in New York, north of Albany.

In one of the Revolution's most critical battles, Burgoyne's army met defeat at Saratoga on October 17, 1777. However, control of the Champlain Valley did not officially return to the Americans until the surrender of Cornwallis and the British retreat to Canada four years later.

With the peace of independence in 1783, commerce soon returned to Lake Champlain. The logging industry and sawmills flourished with the aid of rivers and streams. Products like fur, meat, fish, grain, paper, wool, potash, and livestock traveled down the lake to Canada in exchange for manufactured goods and salt. As a neutral country during the Napoleonic Wars between France and Britain, America boomed with enough trade to stir Europe's resentment. In retaliation for insults to its hard-won independence, such as impressments of American ships, the U.S. Embargo of 1807 insulated the country's resources. By 1809 trade restrictions applied only to Britain and France, and when the Non-Intercourse Act expired, Britain

alone refused to lift its blockade on American shipping—an act of aggression that led the United States to declare war in June of 1812.

Once again, Lake Champlain took up its place in American military history, as a major shipbuilding program began in the city of Vergennes, Vermont. The area provided plenty of timber and a large waterfall to power gristmills, sawmills, and forges. Lieutenant Thomas Macdonough and his men saw little action until the morning of September 11, 1814, when the Americans spied the enemy off Cumberland Head and took up position in Plattsburgh Bay. Forcing the British to sail against the wind, Macdonough prevailed, thus encouraging the forces toiling on land nearby to also beat back the Redcoats, who made their final retreat to Canada.

With peace restored once again, Lake Champlain's commerce could finally develop unimpeded. The first steamship had already appeared in 1809, replacing ferries propelled by sail or guided by ropes or cables, though a regular schedule of service could only resume after the War of 1812. In the 1820s, when paddle-wheel ferries powered by horses walking in place became popular, six horses ran a boat that carried both passengers and livestock between Charlotte, Vermont and Essex, New York. During the next two decades, the

Samuel de Champlain statue on the Plattsburgh waterfront.

lake's commercial traffic expanded to include twelve different ferries whose routes zigzagged between Vermont and New York, and stretched as far as St. Jean, Québec.

In 1823, the opening of the Champlain Canal between Whitehall and Waterford, New

Shadows along the Lake Road, Adirondacks.

York greatly increased the speed at which mail, goods, and passengers could pass between the lake and the Hudson River. At the lake's northern end, the Chambly Canal guided forest products from the woods of Québec to American markets, using a series of locks to bypass the rapids of the Richelieu. This canal operated for more than a century after its opening in 1843, even though the direction of much economic activity soon turned away from Canada and toward the southern United States. By the 1830s, the great volume of traffic on Lake Champlain had convinced the government to install lighthouses, causing the construction and manning of more than a dozen that lasted until automatic lights replaced them a century later.

As tourism increased, the steamboats became larger, faster, and more luxurious. The Champlain Transportation Company managed a fleet of these "floating palaces" through their heyday and into their retirement. The last of those famous steamers, the *Ticonderoga*, was built in 1906 and ran a route from Westport to Plattsburgh, New York. As profits fell with the increase in automobile traffic, the steamer became a ferry between Burlington, Vermont and Port Kent, New York, then again devolved into a private charter boat. Finally, rescuing the ship from a silent death, Mrs. Watson Webb

operated the *Ticonderoga* for several years before donating it to the Shelburne Museum. The expensive, brilliantly engineered overland trip involved dredging the lake, constructing two dikes, laying rail track, and slowly hauling the steamer with tractors and winches in a journey that took three months during the winter of 1954–55.

Today the *Ticonderoga* is still on display in its landlocked cradle at the museum, where visitors can view this unique relic from Lake Champlain's past. To see the remnants of the lake's role in the French and Indian War, the American Revolution, and the War of 1812, one must dive beneath the waves, where much of this underwater archaeology has already begun.

Culture

Once peace came to the Champlain Valley after centuries of conflict, settlers soon ventured away from the lakeshore, founding cities and towns in every corner of good, fertile land. As of the year 2000, the Lake Champlain Basin had a U.S. population of 541,000 people, while 30,000 lived in Québec. Concentrated in the urban centers of Plattsburgh and Glens Falls, New York, and Rutland and Burlington, Vermont, the basin's inhabitants sustain a diverse array of industries and services. While the region's economy has evolved from its original base in timber, iron ore, potash, and support industries such as farming, shipbuilding, and rail and canal boat transport, the Champlain Valley still thrives with agriculture and natural resource industries. For example, Essex County, New York lays claim to America's only mine for wollastonite—a valuable mineral that replaces asbestos. Paper products, milk, apples, meat, slate, and granite all come from the lake's watershed, as does one third of the maple syrup produced in the United States. While sugaring operations abound in the mountains, forage crops, grains, vegetables, and fruits flourish in the gentle lowlands beside the lake.

Farms cover nearly half of the Missisquoi Bay drainage basin, which spans the international border between Québec and northwestern Vermont. In both the Champlain Islands and Addison County, Vermont, farmers take advantage of the relatively warm climate of the "banana belt" along the shores of Lake Champlain, where the growing season is 45 days longer than at higher elevations inland. Dairy farms, vineyards, and apple orchards all

Addison and Grand Isle counties are known for apple production.

benefit from the valley's milder winters. By selling their products at nearby farmers' markets, co-ops, and restaurants, many of these businesses fuel the growing demand for fresh, local food grown with sustainable methods. NOFA-Vermont, the state's organic oversight agency, has seen the number of certified farms

rise from 78 to 543 since 1993. Even as fewer people overall pursue agriculture for a living, this open land still supports the region's cultural heritage and creates a marketable image of the Lake Champlain Basin—a task crucial to the growing service economy.

Today, more than one third of the basin's population works in service industries like retail, health, legal, education, and tourism. Although the manufacturing sector has decreased in importance—a trend consistent across the United States—the Lake Champlain Basin still boasts a diverse economy thanks to the strength of its agriculture, forestry, and construction industries. These traditional ways of life not only create valuable products, but also maintain the pastoral image that attracts tourists to the region. Since the end of the Revolutionary War, the tourism industry has steadily grown from the grand pleasure boats of the nineteenth century to the kite boarders, bass fishermen, and ice climbers of today. The Adirondacks and the Green Mountains attract hikers, photographers, and skiers, while boaters of all descriptions travel the lake and its numerous tributaries.

Several networks of trails crisscross the region, including the Long Trail, a hiking route that runs the length of Vermont; the 1,200 miles of trails that comprise Lake Champlain Bikeways; and the Lake Champlain Paddlers' Trail, which supports human-powered boating with more than 30 campsites and access points along the lake. With so many support organizations, the region promises activities for people of all abilities and ambitions. Intrepid hikers may aspire to join the Adirondack Forty-Sixers by climbing all of the High Peaks over 4,000 feet. For a less strenuous adventure, a family may follow a continuous bike path all the way from the Burlington waterfront to the Cut—a gap in the old rail causeway between Colchester and South Hero. In addition to supplying a boundless arena for outdoor recreation, the Lake Champlain Basin offers many urban possibilities.

As the largest population center in the region, Burlington, Vermont is a dynamic city of 40,000 people who live alongside the University of Vermont's nearly 10,000 students. The Church Street Marketplace, an outdoor pedestrian mall, contains unique shops, chain stores, restaurants, art galleries, and theaters. Not far from the Burlington Boathouse, Per-

kins Pier, and Waterfront Park, the ECHO Center studies the marine ecology of Lake Champlain and educates the public about its aquatic plants, invertebrates, and 81 known species of fish. This combination of local businesses, museums, and historic architecture appears at a smaller scale throughout the basin. The famous ski town of Stowe, the fly-fishing mecca of Manchester, and Middlebury, Vermont—home of Middlebury College—all lie

The Church Street Marketplace in Burlington, Vermont is a hub of retail and business activity.

within the lake's watershed. In addition to fueling the region's economy with jobs and product sales, local businesses such as Lake Champlain Chocolates, Ben and Jerry's, the Vermont Teddy Bear Company, and Otter Creek Brewing entertain tourists with their unique goods and factory tours. New York attracts visitors to the quaint lakeside towns of Westport and Essex, and to the Olympic Sports Complex in Lake Placid, which hosted the 1932 and 1980 Winter Games. Lake George, which drains into Champlain via La Chute River, has its own rich military history, lakeside attractions, and handsome summer homes that define the character of the basin's southwestern corner.

All who visit or live in this wonderful place recognize the unique history, culture, and ecology of the basin. In an effort to preserve the ecosystems, memories, and artifacts of Lake Champlain, many museums display and interpret the region's past. The Shelburne Museum has preserved buildings from early Anglo settlement to the 1950s, as well as a lighthouse, passenger train, and the side-wheel steamer, *Ticonderoga*. A short way to the south, the Lake Champlain Maritime Museum focuses on the lake's naval and commercial history. A great number of downtowns and individual buildings belong to the National Register of Historic Places, while many local historical soci-

The Lois McClure *under full sail on a bright day.*

eties also collect documents, photographs, and genealogies from their towns.

In addition to these efforts to preserve the basin's human past, scientific labs and countless volunteers strive to maintain the lake's natural balance of nutrients and species. In recent years, invasive plants and animals such as water chestnuts, Eurasian milfoil, and purple loosestrife have out-competed Champlain's native species. Zebra mussels, which are particularly damaging, can clog water intake pipes and cover every inch of shipwrecks and other underwater artifacts. Posing another environmental threat, excess phosphorus from urban runoff and agricultural fertilizer can cause toxic blue-green algae blooms. Thankfully, many people devote their time to keeping Lake Champlain and its basin healthy and clean. The lake affects thousands of lives, whether one drinks from a city water system, depends on its rivers to feed crops and livestock, or merely kayaks a stretch of rapids one weekend a year. While its waters mark a state boundary, Lake Champlain also crosses an international border, uniting people from every corner of the basin under a common human and ecological history.

Blue heron.

Sources

Beach, Allen Penfield. *Lake Champlain as Centuries Pass.* Basin Harbor, Vermont: Basin Harbor Club and the Lake Champlain Maritime Museum, 1994.

Hill, Ralph Nading. *Lake Champlain: Key to Liberty.* Taftsville, Vermont: The Countryman Press, 1976.

"Lake Champlain Basin Atlas." Lake Champlain Basin Program, 2004. <http://www.lcbp.org/>

"Shipwrecks and History." Lake Champlain Maritime Museum. <http://www.lcmm.org/>

Photo Credits

Photographer Websites

Paul O. Boisvert: www.pauloboisvert.com

John David Geery: www.johndavidgeery.com

Carl Heilman: www.carlheilman.com

Robert Lyons: www.robertlyonsphotography.com

Brian Mohr: www.EmberPhoto.com

David Seaver: www.davidseaver.com